Is this a book about customer service?

Yes... *but more than that...*

...it offers a fresh, easy and natural way
to provide great customer service...

...and...

it takes you 'out-of-the-box',
to see how this exciting approach to customer service
can benefit *all* your relationships!

So really, it's a book about making your work
and life more enjoyable!

Philip Maggs is currently Chief Executive of Keyturn Training. As a founding partner he has been largely responsible for spearheading the growth of Keyturn into the respected organisation it is today. Personally devoted to high standards of customer service, he has delivered numerous training programmes and seminars on the subject. He has also authored and edited training material, books and articles across a range of subject matter. His smooth-flowing and insightful writing style is sprinkled with humour, making content enjoyable, entertaining, informative and stimulating.

Keyturn Training was established in 1990 by Philip Maggs and David Maggs and has grown to become one of the leading training and development companies within the UK, as well as working further afield for international clients. Customer service is one of Keyturn's areas of specialist activity. Consistently modelling high standards of customer service themselves, Keyturn's team members have helped hundreds of clients to maximise their success through the development of customer service awareness, activities and attitudes.

Care to be different?

Care to be different?

Easy ways to make your work *and life*
more enjoyable...

...explored through a humorous collection of
real-life customer service stories!

Philip Maggs

KEYTURN

Unlocking Potential

Keyturn Training Limited, Inner Lodge, Dunchurch Park, Rugby Road, Dunchurch, Rugby, Warwickshire, United Kingdom, CV22 6QW

Tel: 01788 815500; Fax: 01788 816662;
Email: pjm@keyturn-training.co.uk; www.keyturn-training.co.uk

Dedication

I dedicate this book to my father, David Maggs, who has been a
source of creative inspiration for this project and many others.
He has always believed in me, encouraged me,
and supported me in all I have done.
Thank you Dad.

Special Acknowledgements:

To Peter Campbell-Barker for his original thinking, humour and artistic
talent, which created the majority of the illustrations in 'Care to be
different?'

To my brothers, Chris and Joe, who share my sense of humour and interest
in writing and have provided extensive analysis and feedback to improve the
quality of this work

To Andy Dernie and Louise Lewis who, as Directors of Keyturn Training have
supported me in the production and publishing of 'Care to be different?'
Their approach to work and life models the content of this book and I am
very grateful to have them as colleagues.

Further Acknowledgements:

Grateful thanks is given to several others who have provided input to this
work at various stages of development, Dave C, Dave M, Fiona, Jean, Lesley,
Nikki, Pete, Rachel, Robert, Sue – thank you to you all.

A note from the author...

Thank you for reading 'Care to be different?'

If you're looking forward to the stories, you may like to go straight to page 29, where they start.

If you're keen to explore how to make your work **and life** more enjoyable, you may prefer to read Part 1 first, as this will give you the opportunity of putting in place a valuable foundation on which to build.

However you choose to read and use this book, I hope you enjoy it!!

Philip Maggs

Contents

Part 1 – Getting the right foundation to enable you to enjoy your work *and life*

Part 2 – Eight easy ways to make life more enjoyable for you and your customers
- explored through a humorous collection of real-life customer service stories

Part 3 – Things you may find helpful, interesting and perhaps enjoyable

Part 1
Getting the right foundation to enable you to enjoy your work *and life*

What is good customer service?
- a rainbow of definitions

It's always fascinating to hear groups of people from different organisations, discussing their unique perspectives on a given topic. Working with Keyturn Training, it's been my privilege to gain insights from hundreds of such groups on the topic of 'customer service'. Here's a colourful selection of definitions that people have come up with in response to the question: "What is good customer service?"

~~~~~~

It's what the customer thinks it is – if you see things from their perspective, and meet or exceed their expectations, then you've done a good job

Professionalism, in all my business interactions

It's an 'attitude of quality', expressed in all I think, say, and do

It's giving people what they've paid for

It's giving a good reception to everyone who comes to me for something, whether that be a purchase, information, a bit of advice, a listening ear, comfort, a favour, or a helping hand. You never know when you might be looking for something from them! So give as you would like to receive

Smiling from the inside out, and acting in line with that smile

It's about giving people enjoyable experiences

It's about understanding customers' real needs and expectations, and meeting them whenever reasonably possible

Getting things right for the customer, first time, every time

It's about adding care to service – people appreciate good efficient service, but being cared for is like the icing on the cake – and when service doesn't always go to plan, care goes a long way to keep things running smoothly

Giving people value for money

Going the extra mile

What is good customer service?
- the correct definition

With so many alternative definitions of good customer service being put forward, the obvious question to ask is: "So which one's right?"

It could be argued that all of them are in their own way, and that customer service is different things to different people. In a general sense I would accept that. However, in my quest to help people reach high standards of customer service I believe that one definition in particular stands out. If taken on board and applied consistently, it will result in the happiest customers, the happiest people, and the most successful organisations.

Here it is:

Good customer service is an 'attitude of quality',

expressed in all I think, say, and do

And what exactly is an 'attitude of quality'?

An 'attitude of quality' is a _desire_

to get things right for the benefit of my customer

Who is my customer anyway?
- the short answer

EVERYONE!

Who is my customer anyway?
- the longer answer

Did you agree with the 'short answer'? At first glance, most people find it difficult to accept the idea of viewing EVERYONE as a 'customer'.

However, I hope you're willing to think outside-of-the-box, and consider the exciting possibilities of this approach.

Here's why I think it makes sense to regard EVERYONE as a 'customer'...

Our lives are full of all kinds of interactions with other people. Sometimes these interactions involve someone buying something – a traditional 'customer'. But apart from products or services which they can buy, people need and want many other things from each other: time, attention, information, advice, support, partnership, recommendation, introductions, opportunity to work, loan of equipment, and so on.

I believe that each and every time someone comes to me for something they need or want (whether they are paying money for it or not) there is an opportunity to respond pleasantly, helpfully and efficiently. And that's what I aim to do! There's an interaction in which they receive something from me, and in that sense they become a 'customer', and I am providing customer service.

Most of the time I don't consciously think of it as 'customer service', but simply as 'giving as I would like to receive'. That's a traditional value that holds good through all types of circumstance, and I recommend it wholeheartedly.

You probably know someone for whom nothing seems to be too much trouble. Maybe that's you? My desire is to encourage people to practice customer service in all aspects of life, so that it becomes a natural characteristic.

If everyone works on this basis, giving great 'customer service' in all kinds of situations, overall we'll create a much more cheerful environment in which to work and live.

To my mind, this has got to be good!

What do *you* think?

'Being cheerful'
- a great foundation for great customer service

"Being cheerful keeps you healthy"
– Ancient Hebrew Proverb

I believe *'Being cheerful'* always has a positive effect on health and well-being. Isn't that true throughout human experience?

A new-born baby is subjected to a constant procession of grinning faces, each trying to elicit some sort of response from the new arrival. And sure enough, the baby soon learns to smile. The baby is happy, and we are happy because the baby is happy.

As we grow up we instinctively move towards those experiences that make us feel good. We also learn what makes others feel good, and when someone is feeling down we will often try to cheer them up.

We like people who have a cheerful outlook, who have something positive to say. We're less keen on those who moan all the time, because they often drag others down with them.

Humour is a big part of our daily lives; it oils communication and relationships, and is often used to lighten things up. We like friends who make us laugh, and on those occasions when we just can't stop laughing, we finally emerge from the experience feeling a whole lot better!

Of course, it's not always possible to be cheerful in life. But whenever difficulties do surface, in their many forms, it's always great advice to focus on returning to a cheerful disposition, at the earliest, appropriate opportunity!

'Being cheerful' feels better... and it is better, for your heart, mind and body!

But that's not all. Your cheerfulness will also rub off on others. You don't have to work at it; it happens naturally and automatically!

That's why *'Being cheerful'*, is the simple, but profoundly strong foundation on which this book is built! If you set out to 'Be cheerful', you'll find yourself enjoying the way you provide customer service, in all kinds of 'customer' interactions. You'll want more of the same, and in this way 'Being cheerful' will energise your desire to continue down the route of consistently providing great customer service.

And your customers will not only appreciate the way you are, they'll also take some of your cheerfulness into the next interaction *they* have.

What do you think? Maybe you already work this way.

'Being cheerful' puts a completely new perspective on customer service, and if you decide to adopt it as your foundation, you'll find yourself enjoying your work and life a whole lot more.

Does *'Being cheerful'* appeal to you?

'Being cheerful'
- a dynamic foundation for outstanding team performance

'Being cheerful' is a brilliant foundation for great customer service. It sets you up with the right attitude, and everything else flows from there...

That's true, even if you're the only one doing it!

But one person cannot be everywhere and cover everything. And of course, it's harder to keep being cheerful if those around you are not doing the same thing. So for really outstanding performance, you'll need a team who work well together.

Here's the good news...

If you want the organisations you are part of to be successful in whatever it is they do, **this book is dynamite!**

Why?

Simply because whenever a group of people apply the 'Being cheerful' principle together, the organisation they are part of becomes healthier, stronger, and fitter to achieve its purpose.

But here's the crunch. Even if everyone in your organisation has a copy of this book, the decision to make a difference has to start somewhere. It will start with an individual. How about you?

Care to be different?

Care to be different?
-the obvious crucial question

Of course 'Care to be different?' is a crucial question. And your response to it will determine how far this book becomes of value to you.

It's a question you can begin to answer now.

In fact, you *are* beginning to answer it now... because already there will be a response forming in your heart and head to what you are reading about 'Being cheerful.'

Your heart will be providing a 'felt' response. Whether or not you're happy with your work and life right now, you may be picking up a sense that things could be better. The idea of 'Being cheerful' seems appealing, so you're feeling drawn to embrace it.

Your head will be providing a 'considered' response. This is about whether or not you believe 'Being cheerful' will work for you. If you can see a logical end result that will make things better, you may decide to take steps in that direction by a decision of the will.

So what's your answer to the 'Care to be different?' question? Hopefully it's positive! Would you like to explore further?

How much do you really want things to be different?

Care to be different?
- the hidden crucial question

'Care to be different?' is essentially a question about desire.

The degree to which you care, the degree to which you want things to be different, and the degree to which you are prepared to make that difference... will all be determined by desire. In other words, how much do you really want it?

Of course, desire is a word which has already featured prominently in our definition of good customer service:

> *Good customer service is an 'attitude of quality',*
> *expressed in all I think, say, and do*

> *An 'attitude of quality' is a <u>desire</u>*
> *to get things right for the benefit of my customer*

Your ability to give good customer service is also determined by desire: how much you really *want* to give it!

So, if we're on the right track, desire is going to be fundamental to your success. Which brings us to the *hidden* crucial question:

What drives desire?

Desire is rooted in feelings. We all have an inbuilt instinct (or desire) to move towards enjoyable feelings or those things that will bring us enjoyable feelings.

When we tap into this understanding of how we, as human beings are designed, we can harness the power of desire to perform better, and enjoy work and life more.

When things are going well, enjoyable feelings provide powerful motivation to keep us moving in our chosen direction.

When things are not going so well, enjoyable feelings desert us, and three possibilities arise. The first is that we become despondent, disillusioned, disinterested and even depressed. Clearly this is not good. The second possibility is that we start moving in a different direction, where we believe we will again be able to experience enjoyable feelings. This may be good, especially if we have thought things through and made a conscious decision to do this. On the other hand it may be we are just following the path of least resistance, which may or may not lead us to a better place. The third possibility is that we stay focused on our chosen direction, putting our need for enjoyable feelings to one side for a period of time.

In this latter case we are entering a state of deferred enjoyment, and another strong human characteristic kicks in: determination!

Determination is vital when things don't go so well and enjoyable feelings desert us. It is capable of carrying us through incredible hardship when necessary.

Determination is based on keeping our eyes fixed on an end goal. And interestingly enough, our level of determination always relates to the level of enjoyable feelings which we believe will come our way as a result of achieving that goal.

There are a range of enjoyable feelings which we may seek. People are different and situations are different. But the common denominator is enjoyment. However we choose to express it, we are all seeking enjoyment.

Even when we make sacrifices for the sake of others, and forego more obvious enjoyment, we are actually enjoying the deep satisfaction of doing what we believe to be the right thing. There is nothing wrong with this. It's how we're designed!

So to summarise:

You and I will perform much better, and more consistently, when we are working in harmony with our powerful, natural, in-built, motivational capability.

We do this by taking control of desire, and deciding to focus on enjoyment: 'Being cheerful'.

Our circumstances are often not what we would choose but we can always choose how we respond to our circumstances.

If you decide to adopt 'Being cheerful' as *your* foundational state, it will place you at the right starting point. It will focus you on the goal of *enjoying* what you do and will trigger feelings of enjoyment as you begin to take action.

Care to be different?
- enjoying exploring

If you've answered the question: 'Care to be different?' with a resounding or tentative 'Yes!'...what happens next?

Simply put, you start behaving differently. Firstly, by 'Being cheerful' in all your interactions. Secondly, by finding ways to make these interactions even more enjoyable for your customers. And of course, as you explore different ideas and opportunities, *you* continue to focus on enjoying what *you're* doing!

The customer service stories highlight eight easy ways to make life more enjoyable for you and your customers

You'll notice that the 'Care to be different?' question appears at the end of each story, along with a number of other questions which you may enjoy exploring.

Your response to the crucial 'Care to be different?' question will underpin your answers to the other questions. After reading about the customer service misdemeanours in each story, 'Care to be different?' asks whether you want to ensure you are not found guilty of the same 'crimes'!

The other questions, if you 'care' to consider them, are posed to stimulate constructive and creative thinking; to spark off ideas and maybe discussion. They're not designed to make you feel uncomfortable, or to try and direct you down any particular avenue of thought. There are many ways to provide good customer service, and you'll identify many ways of improving things, just as a result of giving it some thinking time.

In my experience, the quality of customer service I give improves when I spend time thinking about it. Simply put:

If I think about it, I do it better!

I'm sure you'll find the same.

Opposite the questions is a notes page, provided for jotting down:
- things that strike you as important
- things you have realised about yourself
- ways you would like to change
- specific actions you could take or want to take
- ways in which you can make a difference
- specific things related to your own role and activities.

However much effort you choose to put in to make a difference, always remember providing great customer service is about being cheerful, having fun, and making work and life more enjoyable for you and the people you interact with.

So where possible choose to make simple changes, and don't try to do too much in one go. Often one new action at a time is the best way forward. Once one new behaviour becomes integrated into your approach and activities try adding another.

Enjoy exploring!

Part 2
Eight easy ways to make life more enjoyable for you and your customers

... you'll be pleased to hear that dressing up as a jester and learning to juggle isn't one of them... although if it appeals...

1

Enjoy making people feel comfortable

19 ½ minutes

- exploring ways to keep a customer waiting

Who likes queuing!? It's certainly not *my* favourite pastime! You don't know how long you're going to be kept waiting; you often don't know why you're being kept waiting; you feel frustrated; you feel stressed... I could go on. Of course it's unreasonable to expect a queueless society, so we put up with queues as a 'necessary evil'.

But here's the thing: 'Is it the queuing that's the problem, or the way we are treated when we queue?' I recently attended an appointment that brought this question sharply into focus...

~~~~~~

Hospitals have always filled me with dread, and whenever I have to go into one my main aim is to leave again as quickly as possible.

This has often been disconcerting for hospitalised friends and relatives who have spent the day looking forward to some company; within a few minutes of my arrival, they have usually been treated to a bunch of grapes, a glimmer of interest, and a clean pair of heels.

Inevitably, the day came when I had to go into hospital for some investigations myself.

On my first visit, I was horrified to learn from my consultant that my condition would be very likely to involve a long sequence of further visits! My instinctive reaction was to immediately focus on getting out of that hospital as fast as possible, as if my life depended upon it. (Ironically, the reverse was probably true!)

In my desperation to depart, I failed to present myself for one of the tests which my consultant had booked for me. I subsequently received a letter reprimanding me for my non-attendance of this appointment, and instructing me to return on a new date. I felt like a naughty schoolboy being put in detention for missing lessons!

Accompanied by my usual feelings of dread, and a queasy stomach, I reported back to the hospital on the date instructed, at 9.00 am.

I'm not sure what was causing me the greater stress - anticipating the pain associated with the test, or the fear of receiving further admonishment for my misdemeanour. The only pleasing thing about the appointment was the time; at least I would be in early, avoid waiting around, and achieve a quick exit!

But I had not accounted for the nocturnal exploits of the receptionist's nephew!!

Having arrived at the hospital in good time, I joined the queue of worried and unhealthy-looking people waiting to book in at reception.

As I waited, I began to observe the activities taking place behind the reception desk. This was a deliberate strategy on my part, to avoid focusing any more than necessary on the conversations of other queue members, who seemed intent on vocalising descriptive detail of their ailments, with no regard for the churnings occurring in my stomach.

There appeared to be two receptionists on duty, but one of them had his position clearly marked as closed, and kept his head down to avoid eye contact with queue members at all costs. There were occasional signs of movement, but nothing that gave rise to the hope that he might become aware of the growing queue, let alone help to decrease it.

The other receptionist, to be fair, was doing a valiant job of dispersing sick and gloomy people down long corridors to the various departments of the hospital.

That was, until her phone rang...

Immediately she picked it up, and launched into a highly animated conversation with an individual who she was clearly pleased to hear from. It was as if the queue had disappeared from her line of sight.

But we could still see her! And hear her! We were all provided with intimate details of the night-time activities of her nephew, none of which incidentally, had anything to do with ill health. The call was clearly a personal one!

The queue stood stoutly and silently awaiting a resumption of service. Even those intent on discussing the details of their illnesses had assumed a disgruntled quietness.

In turn, we went through the motions of looking ourselves up and down to check for signs of temporary invisibility, but we all knew this was futile. The reality was we were being treated as unimportant.

We were being ignored!

No one was happy. No one complained. No one said anything.

It was a model enactment of the great British queue; each person resolutely holding their place in line, as if competing in a 'who can hold out the longest' challenge.

After what seemed to be an eternity, the 'head down' receptionist glanced up, and inadvertently caught the eye of the first person in the queue. With a sigh and body language that made it obvious he didn't want to get involved, he found himself forcing out the question: "Do you have an appointment?"

The person at the front of the queue stepped forward, offering the reluctant receptionist an engaging smile. The receptionist was not about to cave in.

On the contrary he steeled himself, working the lines of his face into a stern expression, topped with an air of disapproval and superiority. Once again, school-day memories were invoked; I now felt as if I was presenting myself at the headmaster's office awaiting my turn to be cross-examined. A sense of guilt began to envelope me.

Gradually each member of the queue took their turn speaking with the 'headmaster', and each was duly dispatched down one corridor or another.

Meanwhile, the original receptionist became even more fully engaged in her personal call. No guilty feelings there, I thought.

Surprisingly, the second receptionist seemed to have no particular issue with his colleague's 'personal call'. Any annoyance he may have felt, served only to fuel his irritation with people in the queue, especially those whose registration details were anything less than straight forward.

I had been queuing for 19½ minutes when my turn came. I know because I had been studying the face of my wrist watch at regular intervals since my initial arrival.

The purpose of my visit was quickly confirmed, and thankfully without any reference to my previous non-attendance, I was directed to disappear down a long corridor. I obediently followed my instructions and eventually emerged into a waiting room already occupied by five other people.

It was here I learnt that everyone present had been given appointment times of 9.00am, and that treatment was being administered on a first come, first served basis.

This discovery was quite annoying, particularly given the frustrating 19½ minutes I had already spent at the other end of the corridor.

But this 'queue' was different. A friendly and enthusiastic nurse made that difference with his smile, and general helpfulness. He made sure everyone had a seat, and that we all knew what was going on. He was sensitive as he went about weighing us in turn and quite simply, made us feel comfortable!

I won't say it became a pleasure to be there - far from it - but in small ways this nurse was making a big difference!

When I trekked back down the corridor some 45 minutes later, there was a queue waiting at reception. In passing, I offered a smile of encouragement to some of the people who stood within it, noting that the 'headmaster' receptionist was nowhere to be seen, and the other receptionist was engaged in an animated phone conversation.

Surely, I reflected, that couldn't still be the same call...?

Care to be different?

How would you describe the way I was treated in the two different queuing scenarios?

What would you do if you were on a personal call and a customer was waiting?

How long do you think it's reasonable to keep a customer waiting?

When queuing is necessary, what do you think are the best ways of making sure it's not an unpleasant experience?

When do you ever keep people waiting? Do you think that's ok? Could you make things better for people who end up waiting for your attention?

Who do you imagine enjoyed their day the most: the receptionist taking her personal call, the receptionist keeping his head down, or the helpful nurse?

Care to be different?
- enjoy making people feel comfortable

Notes...

2

Enjoy putting 'heart' into your words and actions

Lip service
- the art of saying the right things in the wrong way

Whenever we are spoken to, we automatically listen to the tone of voice much more sensitively than we listen to the words. This is because the tone tells us a lot about the 'heart' of the person who is addressing us - where they are really coming from, and whether they are sincere. Obviously, an ill-chosen selection of words can be very upsetting, but more often than not, it is an unpleasant or ill-fitting tone of voice, that can throw us off our stride – as was the case with one of my best mates, when he tried to plan a rather special evening...

~~~~~~~~~~~~~~~~~~~~~~~~~~~~~~~~~~~~~~~

It's not often that Jim does the 'romantic stuff', so when he told me he'd arranged to take Wendy out for a 'cosy evening meal', I was certainly taken by surprise!

I was less surprised when I asked which restaurant he had booked, to discover this was a detail which Jim considered unnecessary. His plan was to travel out of town and find a venue that neither of them had been to before, to make the evening a bit more special.

I pointed out that it was still possible to book a table at a venue they had not been to before, but Jim, being Jim, was undeterred: "We're bound to come across somewhere nice", he unreasonably concluded, and subsequently did not trouble himself to research the matter further.

It was a cold and snowy day when he picked Wendy up, and as luck would have it the heater in Jim's car chose that very same day to withdraw its services. Nevertheless, Jim stuck to his plan to drive out of town, and headed off into the countryside.

Jim was not quick to confess that he had not actually booked a table, but as he drove slowly through the third village that they came to, his eyes scanning hopefully up every side street they passed, the admission became unavoidable. A further snow shower was now restricting visibility, and Wendy's demeanor was beginning to match the temperature! "I thought you knew where you were going," she snapped!

As Jim turned his head to point out that her attitude was not helping, he saw *'The Eatery'*. A fairly small but tastefully designed sign, hung invitingly at the far end of the side street they were passing. This timely observation saved Jim from inadvertently bringing the evening to a swift and premature conclusion!

Quickly finding a parking place in the quiet street, the couple got out of Jim's car and silently walked the few paces necessary to reach *'The Eatery'*. Pausing briefly to observe the menu placed in the window, they were soon enjoying the warm air meeting their chilled faces, as they passed through the welcoming front entrance.

Jim's eye was immediately drawn across the room to rest on a mouth-watering display of sweets, spread out in glass-fronted cooling cabinets. In many ways he felt his evening was already complete. By contrast, his partner's eye was immediately drawn to the beautifully co-ordinated décor and bright, fresh paintwork.

"Looks like a new place", Wendy commented, looking around in a satisfied manner. Jim briefly wrenched his drooling gaze from the tempting array of sweets to acknowledge the pleasantness of their surroundings with a manly grunt. He was about to refocus on a particularly sumptuous chocolate gateau, when Wendy's nudge sent his gaze across to the 'Under New Management' notice; "I expect they've refurbished it", she suggested.

Jim took a moment to look around more thoughtfully. He could see that great care had gone into creating a warm and relaxing environment. Table areas were tastefully divided to give some privacy to diners and he looked forward to a pleasant evening ahead... hopefully topped off with some of that chocolate gateau!

"See, I knew it would work out okay", Jim said, in his mind. Outwardly, he contented himself with a warm smile that contained just a hint of smugness.

Although he disguised it well, in his opinion, Jim became aware that Wendy was studying his expression with some suspicion. Skillfully, he manipulated his facial muscles through a series of rapid contortions, in response to an imaginary itch just under his right eye. Under this cover, Jim successfully replaced his smug expression with something more endearing, and the moment passed.

A waiter appeared at the far end of the room to deposit a tray of freshly washed glasses. Placing them on the bar, he suddenly became aware of the couple's presence – at which point he seemed startled, and then disappointed.

He glanced towards a 'Staff Only' door as if weighing up his chances of escape, but then seemed to resign himself to the fact that the couple had not only seen him but were now closely observing his every move.

"Welcome to *'The Eatery'*". The words were good, but they paid no resemblance to any other aspect of the waiter's manner. In fact, had he said "Please will you leave", that would have been more fitting!

"Would you like a table?" he offered, with the enthusiasm of someone who's just been told they've got to work an extra shift without pay. Jim would often take the opportunity to answer a question like that with some witty reply, but this character was so depressing, Jim's usual sharp wit failed him, and he simply murmured a rather weak, "Yes please".

"You can choose one if you like?" suggested the waiter, in his distinctive drone, "And someone will serve you in a minute". Having delivered this statement, the waiter promptly disappeared through the 'Staff Only' door. Jim concluded that he was probably going off duty, and naturally had not wanted his imminent exit to be in any way delayed, certainly not by a customer!

Had there been alternative options to hand, Jim and Wendy may have reconsidered their decision to eat at the establishment. But there were no realistic alternatives.

Hoping the departed waiter's attitude was not representative of all the staff at *'The Eatery'*, they chose one of the pre-set tables, sat down, picked up the brand new menus and began to lick their lips at the tempting array of dishes on offer. (Actually, Wendy being rather more refined, it was just Jim that did the lip-licking.)

Several minutes passed with no sign of any other waiters appearing, but Jim and Wendy were in no rush. The surroundings were warm and comfortable, and as they watched the light snow still falling in the street, they knew it would be some time before they headed out there again. In the meantime they were pleasurably settled into their own cosy corner.

In this peaceful and relaxing environment, frustrations of the day were quickly melting away, and gazing across the table into his partner's eyes, Jim gave her his most romantic look. Her laugh was slightly disconcerting, but instinctively he knew this was the moment. Jim reached into his pocket...

"ARE YOU READY TO ORDER?" The question came without warning, delivered in the style of an army officer barking a command! The whole atmosphere changed instantly! Lifting his eyes towards this unpleasant intrusion, Jim observed a person looking as though he had rolled out of bed just two minutes earlier, annoyed that his slumber had been disturbed.

"We're not ready to order any food yet", Jim smiled, wondering why he was responding so pleasantly, "But we'll have two glasses of house wine, please".

"MEDIUM OR LARGE?" fired the loud, threatening figure overshadowing the couple's table. His abrupt approach seemed so deliberate that it would not have been unreasonable to assume that his main objective was to disrupt the atmosphere they were settling into and provoke them into an early departure!

"LARGE", Jim blurted out, feeling obligated to respond with immediacy. Strangely, Jim found himself smiling again, but with no response from the waiter, who departed from the table without even so much as a "Thank you".

Upon the silent delivery of the wine, Jim and Wendy placed their food orders, meekly accepting the apparent desire of their host to avoid speech wherever possible. Given his abruptness and volume whenever he did speak, silence was probably preferable. Strangely however, an uncomfortable silence now seemed to be creeping across the whole restaurant. No longer peaceful and relaxing, the mood was... restrictive, not unlike that in the waiting room of a dentist's surgery. Wendy and Jim became very self-conscious of their own voices and their conversation became stilted.

Their selected dishes were duly delivered, with an instruction rather than an invitation: "ENJOY YOUR MEALS!"

Although that had been the couple's full intention on arrival, it now seemed strangely difficult to follow through on. Being *told* to enjoy their meals, produced the opposite effect to that which the speaker had presumably intended.

Or was he just giving them lip service? Did the waiter care whether they enjoyed their meals or not? If he did, he didn't show it!

The final insult came as he scurried past the couple's table, proclaiming the inevitable, "IS EVERYTHING ALRIGHT WITH YOUR MEAL?" It was really a statement rather than a question and he had no intention of stopping to listen to any response. Nothing short of a rugby tackle would have halted him in his tracks!

The food itself tasted good and the place did look the part, but the couple didn't have a sweet (not even Jim), and they've never been there again. The next time they went out, they booked in advance, at a place I recommended. And Jim finally popped the question...

As for 'The Eatery', I believe that it's once again 'Under New Management'!

Care to be different?

"What comes out of the mouth, reveals the heart." Do you agree with this proverb?

How easy is it to find yourself saying the right things in the wrong way; just giving 'lip service' to something?

How would you have responded to these waiters if you had been in Jim's position?

If 'The Eatery' was placed under your management, what are the top three changes you would make?

Why is it that our tone of voice sometimes gives a different message to the words we are using? How can we stop this happening?

How does 'Being cheerful', help you to enjoy putting 'heart' into your words and actions?

Care to be different?
- enjoy putting 'heart' into your words and actions

Notes...

3

Enjoy being sensitive to someone's situation and feelings

A joke too far
- how to find the limit of your customer's patience

Whatever your perspective on a given situation, you can safely bet that someone else will have a different perspective, sometimes wildly different. I find it quite amusing to watch sportspeople debate refereeing decisions; invariably individuals consider decisions to be right or wrong, depending on whether or not those decisions work in their team's favour! Each person, quite naturally, is looking at the situation from their own perspective. And we do this all the time, in all kinds of situations.

For better communication and to raise the bar in providing good customer service, things will generally start to work better when we try to see someone else's perspective. 'Putting ourselves in their shoes,' is another way of saying it. The following story illustrates this vital point very well...

~~~~~~

STOP!

The command appeared on the dashboard of my car in an intimidating manner!

There was no enquiry as to where I was going, the length of my journey, or its purpose. There was no consideration for the implications of failing to reach my destination. Just an unequivocal demand that I put aside my travel priorities and obey the instruction, brazenly parading in front of me!

As it happens, I was simply en route to my local recycling centre, with the intention of diverting past the newsagents on my return journey, to pick up a magazine and a paper.

It may not appear that this was a critical journey at first glance, but its successful accomplishment would have meant I could have enjoyed a rare couple of hours to myself, relaxing in my garden. So it was important to me! And anyway, I take exception to being told what to do by a computer – anytime!

Having expressed my annoyance at being told to 'STOP', and my indignation at the manner in which I was being told… I reluctantly pulled over to the side of the road.

"Is that it!?" I asked my vehicle, impatiently. Whether it didn't like the way I asked the question, or whether it was ill-equipped to reply, no further information was forthcoming, so I resorted to the glove box.

My vehicle has a large glove box, and I make full use of it. Maps, sweets, chocolate, gloves, socks, sunglasses, first aid stuff, pens, small tools, CD's, spare handkerchiefs (and the odd used one), recovery service information, insurance documents – it's all packed in there, and somewhere, usually at the bottom, is the handbook!

On this occasion extracting the handbook involved an additional degree of difficulty, due to the adhesion caused by a recent spillage of fizzy drink. A few weeks earlier I had tried to discourage my young son from bringing his beverage into the car, but he had been keen to experiment with the retractable cup holder, and not wanting to stunt his budding interest in the feats of modern engineering, I had conceded.

Whether the cup was the wrong size or shape, whether the retraction mechanism activated, or whether my son was just clumsy was never established. What was clear, was that the cup was no longer in the holder, and the drink was no longer in the cup. It was in the glove box!

Cup holder designers have a lot to answer for, in my opinion.

After trying half-a-dozen improvised methods of parting bonded materials, I placed my patience on one side and yanked the manual from its internment! Half of the back cover remained resolutely attached to the interior of the glove box, where as far as I know, it remains to this day!

It did not surprise me to observe that a number of pages within the manual were also stuck together, with varying degrees of strength. It *did* surprise me, that the section entitled 'Digital display commands', was *not* stuck together!

Although still taking some exception to the word *'commands'*, I found what I was looking for. "If the display commands 'STOP', pull over immediately and activate secondary digital display."

Easier said than done! After activating a number of other things, including the windscreen wipers and fog lights, the secondary digital display appeared and I found myself staring at a computer-generated image of a nail entering the surface of a tyre.

Turning off the engine, I got out of the car, and began an inspection of each of the four tyres in turn. A passer-by took it upon himself to interject:

"You've got a puncture mate!"

His brash, 'know-it-all' manner instantly rubbed me up the wrong way. "This one, at the front", he continued, as if the fact that I was currently inspecting a rear tyre indicated a degree of incompetence that he had not previously encountered. I thanked him through gritted teeth and he went on his way, clearly feeling he had done his good deed for the day!

Making my way around to the offending tyre I could see that it was unhealthy. There was no obvious nail as per the graphic on my dashboard, but there was a distinct lack of air. I nonchalantly kicked the wheel. I'm not sure what that achieves, but I've seen other guys do it, and it seemed appropriate.

I did not relish the idea of changing the wheel at the roadside, so I returned to the driver's seat and restarted the engine. Immediately the onboard computer tried to resume control and flicked its command back in front of my face: 'STOP'.

I smiled at it, defiantly, and drove off down the street!

The car felt odd to drive, understandably, but I knew I was within a couple of miles of a tyre service centre, and I enjoyed establishing my authority over the computer!

On arrival, I explained my predicament to the helpful looking fitter who approached me. He listened politely, then walked over to my vehicle.

"You don't want to be driving on that!" he proclaimed, "You wouldn't believe how many people drive in here on 'flats', ruining their tyres and the rims too. Clueless, they are!"

I wondered whether it was his regular custom to greet people with a statement of the obvious, followed by an insult! He was clearly oblivious to the fact that he had done either and instead was occupying himself with a closer inspection of the damage. I stood behind him reflecting on my apparent stupidity and ignorance!

The fitter ran his hands around the offending tyre several times before declaring his verdict. "Must be your lucky day," he quipped, "You've not damaged the rim and I think the tyre's okay too, apart from this nail of course!" He chuckled at his joke as he pointed to the offending item which he had managed to locate.

Strangely, I did not see the funny side and also failed to agree with his suggestion that I was having a 'lucky day'! Still oblivious to my feelings, he carried on confidently, "Should be just a puncture repair. Do you want to leave it with us?"

"I'd rather wait if that's ok", I replied. "Sure. But I hope you're not in a hurry", he laughed jovially. I was not amused, and considered venturing down the route of explaining what I had hoped to do that morning, and why in fact I *was* in a hurry of sorts. But I sensed I would be wasting my breath. Besides which, if I kept him talking, I would only be delaying him from starting work on my punctured tyre.

As it turned out, he was not short of things to delay him starting!

I was directed to wait in the reception area, where I found a number of magazines, full of pictures of exquisite cars that I could not afford. I browsed through them once, then once again as the time passed slowly by.

I'd had just about enough of torturing myself in this manner, when my fitter walked through the door. Good timing, I thought.

"Could I have your keys please sir".

"My keys?" I questioned. "Yes sir. Unless you'd like to come and help me push your car into the workshop?" he joked. Again it was not funny, not to me anyway.

"I thought you were already working on it", I exclaimed. "Not started yet, sir", returned the casual reply, with a slight shrug of the shoulders. He seemed surprised that I would be thinking otherwise. I handed over my keys, realising that I should have been alert to the lack of progress being made, given that they had remained in my possession up to now.

There were coffee making facilities on the far side of the counter but no-one had invited me to help myself and it seemed to me they were probably for the use of staff. Not that I particularly wanted a drink – I was simply looking for something to do. I patiently returned to the magazines and idly began glancing through them for a third time.

It was then that the phone started ringing. Initially, I was thinking: "Why doesn't someone come and answer that? Have they no standards here? That could be an important customer calling in!"

My feelings changed a little when the fitter I believed to be working on my car reappeared. "Surely *your're* not going to answer it!" I felt quite strongly that this would be inappropriate, but probably for the best the words were spoken only in my head.

Without rushing (I don't think anything would have made him rush) my fitter made his way to the phone, commenting: "You just can't get the staff these days, can you?"

I presume he also meant that as a joke, but given the way I was feeling I was happy to concur with his comment as an accurate statement of fact.

As I continued to wait, I became aware that the incoming call did indeed seem to be from an important customer - one of their business accounts in fact - and it appeared there had been some sort of accident which required an immediate response. I was intrigued to know quite what this establishment's concept of an 'immediate response' was, but I was about to find out.

Without increasing actual speed of movement beyond casual, all employees gradually became involved in discussion and activity relating to the 'accident'. Mainly discussion.

I mused that I was probably observing this team of workers in their highest mode of operation. An ingrained pattern of working had obviously evolved over some lengthy period of time, probably years, and clearly the corporate 'mind-set' did not include 'a sense of urgency'. From clocking-on time, to clocking-off time, they were at work. The start and end times never changed. Working faster did not make the day shorter. So they did not work faster. Which is not to say they did not work hard or efficiently. They maintained a steady, casual pace, which was probably a fair input for the rewards they were paid.

But I did have a sense of urgency! And found their lack of pace intensely irritating!

I had no desire to be where I was, and wished to be on my way at the earliest opportunity. The failure of the fitting team to recognize this, let alone respond to it, was becoming a growing problem to me.

My mind set off in another direction, this time reviewing my own actions. Maybe I should have thought things through a little more before driving here. Perhaps I could have obtained roadside assistance quicker. Breakdown recovery would have put the spare wheel on for me, and I could then have arranged to book my vehicle in at my convenience. I could have phoned around for best price. Then again, why didn't I attempt to change the wheel at the roadside myself...

Deep down, I knew the answer to this last consideration. I've never been good with mechanical things. The embarrassing attempt to help a young lady repair the wheel on her pushbike some years earlier, surfaced from my memory as a case in point. I had been obliged to leave her with a twenty pound note to repair the additional damage I had inadvertently caused...

Suddenly I snapped back to reality. This was getting me nowhere! I had been waiting for nearly an hour already and had received no positive information about progress on my vehicle whatsoever. Even now, I didn't know whether work had actually started!

I rose purposefully from my seat and strode across reception towards the workshop door. But as quickly as I had felt energized to make my presence felt, my courage seemed to slip away as I questioned exactly what I intended to say.

At that precise moment the workshop door opened. I swiveled neatly on the spot and walked in the opposite direction, as if pacing the room.

"Are you ok sir?" It was a different fitter, but another friendly voice, which automatically triggered my wholly inappropriate response: "Yes, fine thank you."

I just managed to rectify this inadequacy before the individual disappeared again. "Er... actually, do you think you could check out how long my car will be?" I asked.

"Probably the same length as when it came in."

I admit I was becoming a little over sensitive by this point, and the friendly fellow was only trying to inject some light humour into the day, but this was a joke too far!

"WHAT!?" I exclaimed aggressively, surprising even myself.

The joker jumped visibly, and as a precaution positioned himself closer to the workshop door. "I'm sorry sir. I didn't mean to offend. I'll go and check the situation right away", and he wasted no time disappearing into the workshop, probably imagining I was hot on his heels.

In reality, had he delayed, I probably would have apologised too. But as it was, I reflected that my 'outburst' may have been exactly what was needed! His failure to return within the next couple of minutes led me to reflect that maybe it was not what was needed.

Unsure of my next move, I felt the fight draining from within me, and I'm sad to say I allowed myself to drift into a semi-conscious state of resignation.

I briefly considered returning to the magazines, but decided against it. I stood gazing out of the window instead; I don't know how long I was there.

"All done sir", came a voice from behind me. My original fitter stood with my car keys in his hand, smiling.

"Would you like the offending missile as a souvenir?" he asked, showing me a nail, not unlike that portrayed on my dashboard.

I declined, but managed a polite smile. "So what do I owe you?" I questioned.

"Nothing sir. We don't charge for puncture repairs. Hopefully you'll come back to us when you need your tyres replacing."

That was a pleasant surprise. And sufficient to challenge the entirely negative impression I had formed in my mind. Despite the frustrating wait, I left feeling that if only there had been a bit more consideration for my frustrations, and a bit more communication on progress, I may have appreciated the jovial atmosphere, and the overall service, considerably more than I did.

Care to be different?

How easy is it to see something from someone else's point of view?

Do you sometimes try to put yourself 'in your customer's shoes'? Do you think this is a good thing to do on a regular basis?

How do you go about trying to understand how your customer feels? How can you ensure this is an enjoyable experience?

Given the second fitter's attempts to be pleasant, how do you think he felt about my 'outburst' towards him? If you were that fitter would you be tempted to think, "I won't bother next time!"?

What kind of things influence our thinking, and the subsequent perspectives we adopt?

Do you think we should be willing to consider changing our own perspectives? In what circumstances might this be appropriate?

Are there any current circumstances where you may be able to improve a situation by considering someone else's perspective?

Could I have made things better by looking at things from the fitters' perspective; 'putting myself in *their* shoes'?

Care to be different?
- enjoy being sensitive to someone's situation and feelings

Notes...

4

Enjoy being
on the ball

Reckless smiling
- the 'wisdom' of giving blind reassurance

For all the emphasis placed on being pleasant and cheerful, good customer service would be totally incomplete without efficiency. Providing accurate information, and taking relevant, prompt action, are obviously essential.

The following story demonstrates both the absence and presence of efficiency, within a company I had grown to trust. When an inefficient action wasted a lot of my time, it took a big effort, combining efficiency and the right attitude, to retain my custom...

~~~~~~~~~~~~~~~~~~~~~~~~~~~~~~~~~~~~~

It was good to be speaking to a salesperson who had a big smile on their face!

Not that I could see it, because I was on the phone; but I could *feel* it!

From the moment she came on the line, there was a clear sense of welcome; a positivity and pleasantness, that made me instantly glad I had made the call.

...and try to put a smile into your voice!

"This is the way all calls should be answered", I pronounced to myself. Briefly, an intrusive thought took the liberty of challenging how I answered the phone personally. Having resolved to review my own approach, I returned to the matter in hand...

I use a range of software products and had been a customer of this particular company for some years. I do like their products, but also use software from other suppliers, according to my assessment of what best meets my needs, and what I am prepared to pay.

I had recently been notified of a particular upgrade I could purchase, in respect of a project management program I was using. It was a high quality program, designed for professional use, and I had purchased it from an alternative supplier.

As the upgrade was quite expensive, I thought I'd check out my regular supplier, to see if they had developed anything comparable. On their website, a considerably cheaper product was indeed available, and it appeared to list all the content that I was looking for. My only reservation was that its description read: 'The most powerful home-based project management package on the market'. What exactly did 'home-based' mean?

So I had picked up the phone.

After minimal discussion, the warm and friendly person on the other end of the line was giving me full reassurance that their product was everything I wanted, and more. Not that I wanted the 'more', but most software comes with a large quantity of clever options that you are never likely to use! It seems the development philosophy is: "If we can do it, we include it". Whether it is useful is of secondary importance. Actually, probably not important at all!

Nevertheless, I could feel I was on the verge of a decision. A better price, from a company I had confidence in; and now, as I was being led to believe, a better package too!

The problem was that it was now sounding like one of those 'too good to be true' opportunities, so I decided to double check. "So you are telling me that your product is now better than the professional one that I'm currently using?"

"Most definitely", came the smiling, friendly reply, "And you can try it before you pay for it".

That was fair enough, but what I wanted to avoid was the hassle of loading up all my data onto a new program to 'try it', only to find out that I had wasted my time. After all, my time is valuable. But I felt my 'friend' on the other end of the phone understood that.

I was hooked. I dropped my lingering resistance to buy and gave the go ahead: "Okay, I'll have it."

The salesperson was delighted, and continued to smile as she confirmed the delivery details. She congratulated me on my purchase, and I felt quite pleased with myself. She concluded by wishing me an enjoyable time using my new 'latest edition' product, and I reflected on what a pleasant experience buying can be, if you are served by a friendly person.

I relaxed back in my chair, taking the opportunity to bang my elbow on the filing cabinet which had recently been moved to a new, 'more convenient' position. And the moment was gone.

The next day I received the software by post and excitedly sat down to load it. I was keen to see the improvement and progress promised by the sales person. I did not find it. And it took me the best part of two days to 'not find it'!

Yes, it was good as a home-based product, but as I entered more and more detailed data, it became increasingly clear that this software was not comparable to the professional program I was currently using. Yes, it contained all the relevant features I required, but the degree to which they allowed manipulation of data, was severely limited in key areas.

After investing far too many precious hours in 'trying it out', I finally threw myself back in my chair in exasperation, once again locating that 'conveniently placed' cabinet with my elbow!

Naturally, this served to fire up my exasperation still further, and in this enhanced state of anxiety I called the customer service number, prominently displayed on the software packaging. I was spared the trauma of an automated reply, and instantly felt drawn in by the warm greeting and inviting question: "How can I help you sir?"

Instinctively, I knew the person posing the question was smiling, and momentarily I cautioned myself not to be drawn into the trap of 'feigned friendliness'! After all, this was the same company that had already lured me into purchasing an unsuitable product, using the mask of a smile!!

Adopting a suitably stern manner, I provided an explanation of my problem. The friendly person simply asked if they could look into the matter and call me back.

This seemed reasonable and I gave my assent, despite the attempted protests of my more dramatic side, which still saw the opportunity for creating an epic tale of enticement, betrayal and broken trust!

Without any drama whatsoever, I received a call from the software company later that day, with an apology for the inaccurate assurances given by their salesperson and the intriguing enquiry: "May we ask what we could do to make up for this and ensure you remain a customer?"

While impressed with their desire to compensate in some way, and to retain my custom, I suggested that it was up to them to suggest a course of action that would achieve this. I was further impressed that they were ready for such a reply. They suggested that I keep the project management program for potential back-up use as I saw fit, and offered to upgrade two other software programs that I had previously purchased from them, 'free of charge'.

This was a helpful offer, and on balance a fair solution, in my opinion. A dissenting voice in my head made a final, fleeting attempt to present a conspiracy theory of deepest subterfuge, but it was desperate, and was duly silenced by more rational thought.

Because of the efficient, friendly way in which my complaint had been handled, I believed that this approach was representative of the true ethos of the company.

I accepted the offer and have continued to use and purchase this company's software ever since. I am still greeted with a smile every time I phone. And I enjoy purchasing from them!

As for the misguided salesperson, who blindly reassured me in areas she clearly did not understand, all I can say is that I hope she learned something valuable from her slip-up!

Care to be different?

Of what value is friendliness without efficiency?

How easy is it to fall into the trap of telling someone what you know they want to hear?

How efficient do you think the salesperson was in assuring me I was buying the right product? What could/should she have done differently?

How close do you think the company came to losing my business altogether? Would that have been a big deal for them?

What were the key actions taken by the company to turn the situation around?

If you could do one thing to improve your efficiency, what would it be? Who would it help? Would it help you? Would it make life more enjoyable?

Care to be different?
- enjoy being 'on the ball'

Notes...

5

Enjoy taking a problem off someone's shoulders

Kitchen confusion
-someone else will sort it out

This story is essentially about taking responsibility. You may know of the proverb; 'too many cooks spoil the broth! Sometimes too many people become involved in a situation, when what is needed is for one person to take responsibility for sorting something out. They may well seek advice or information from others, and possibly ask for help in particular areas – but they get the job done! Efficiently and quickly!

This did not happen when my parents took the decision to order a new kitchen. If I may take the liberty of adapting the above proverb; 'too many customer service representatives spoil the delivery'...

~~~~~~

The brand new, shiny modern kitchen was finally ordered!

The news was welcomed by the friends of my parents, who had become weary of subjection to lengthy descriptions of design deliberations, quotation processes and supplier selection!

There followed a 6 week delay before delivery would be made, but anticipation and excitement grew rapidly when my father received the promised phone call from the chosen supplier: "Delivery of your cupboard units will be next Tuesday, at approximately 11am, and the electrical appliances will follow on Wednesday."

It was a clear and simple communication and my parents' expectations were set.

Preparations began in earnest. Existing kitchen cupboards were cleared of all the items that had gradually filled them to capacity over the last 14 years. Deep discussion ensued over the worthiness of a vast range of unused objects and their subsequent fate, and the empty cupboards were cleaned in readiness to be scrapped! (Don't ask!)

On the day of delivery, work resumed to make space in a room next to the kitchen area, sufficient to receive the large delivery that even now would be 'en route' to my parents' home.

Finally we were done! I say 'we', as I had been drafted in to help with lifting the heavier items. After salvaging mugs, conveniently placed in a box which had somehow found its way to a remote position at the back of the garage, we sat back to enjoy a coffee and a well earned rest. We waited in confidence that all would be well.

As it turned out, all was not well!

After a second cup of coffee, my father made a call to enquire if the delivery had been delayed. Carol, a customer service representative, consulted her computer screen and advised that my parents' delivery was under query. My father's expectation of a little more detail was unmet, but Carol did respond positively to his suggestion that she might look into the matter further and call him back.

It was now lunchtime; a few sandwiches were assembled using the severely limited kitchen facilities, and we continued our encampment in my parents' lounge.

It's a comfortable lounge, and we were not under any real threat of survival, but by 4pm we had become strangely distraught.

The non-arrival of the kitchen was obviously disappointing but the lack of communication concerning its non-arrival was particularly irritating.

My mother's emotions of pleasure and excitement had all but disappeared as my father picked up the phone again. He came off the phone at 4.45pm with a headache, and an assurance from Kevin, another customer service representative, that everything would now be delivered tomorrow, although for reasons beyond our understanding there would still be two separate deliveries.

As it turned out, everything was not delivered tomorrow!

The first delivery the next day did consist of most of the required cupboard units, but the delivery note stated that an outstanding 400mm wall unit would follow under separate delivery.

The appliances arrived in due course a couple of hours later, with the exception of the built-in microwave oven, and still no 400mm wall unit. Naturally, my father telephoned customer service. This time, the person on the other end of the line was called Naomi.

Naomi could not coax her computer into life and therefore asked for a description of the missing items. It was not long before she uttered the reassuring words, "I know exactly what you mean". She said she'd put through a manual request for delivery of the correct items the next day. My father was happy and the call came to a reasonably prompt and satisfactory conclusion.

"I know <u>exactly</u> what you mean..."

He was dealing with a large and professional, national company. And the items in question were part of a catalogued range. Surely it was reasonable for him to be cautiously optimistic?

He was pleasantly surprised to receive a delivery early the next day. He was less pleasantly surprised, on removal of the packaging, to discover a microwave oven from a different product range.

A further phone call was required, and to preserve my father's sanity, I took up the mantle. I was put through to yet another customer service representative; Parmdeep.

Having listened to my explanation of the problem in some detail, Parmdeep put me on hold while he did whatever it was that he does on such occasions. He finally returned to ask me if I was sure that I wanted the microwave oven exchanged. I confirmed with some degree of vigour that as the delivered item did not match the main oven, I was indeed sure.

Not content with the level of frustration he had managed to provoke thus far, Parmdeep proceeded to ask me once again to describe the missing microwave oven!

"It's from the same range as the main oven!", I exclaimed, in a slightly embarrassing high pitched voice. "Yes, I know," came the slightly impatient reply, "But our computer system is down and I can't retrieve your information. If you describe the microwave for me so that we can match your needs exactly, we won't make any more mistakes."

The underlying tone seemed to imply that our inability to provide an accurate description was probably the root of the problem!!

I strongly resented that implication.

Nevertheless, I complied and provided the description again. When I heard the words, "I know exactly what you mean", I was less than convinced. "Just give us a couple of days to sort it out", Parmdeep requested.

Two days later there was no sign of a microwave. But a 400mm cupboard unit did arrive, which would have been a step in the right direction… except for the fact that it was a 'floor unit', not a 'wall unit'.

Back on the phone I went and began a conversation with Kevin. At least this was someone my father had spoken to before. But my naïve belief that this might in some way prove to be an advantage was short-lived.

The initial apology was welcomed and accepted. Unfortunately it was followed up by the suggestion that I may not have provided a sufficiently clear description of the type of unit required!

A series of response options passed rapidly through my mind. As a responsible adult, I filtered out those that were largely focused on venting my wrath on the individual who now sat at the other end of the phone.

After a pause of several seconds, I spoke: "Kevin, your company has already made several mistakes with this order and I am very unhappy about the number of calls we are having to make to deal with the confusion. I need you to talk to whoever you need to within your company to sort this out, then someone needs to call me with the solution. If that doesn't happen today, we will seriously consider canceling the whole order."

Reflecting on my largely impromptu speech, I was quite impressed with myself. I had retained a reasonably calm manner, but had been clear and firm about what I wanted. I had slight misgivings about my 'canceling the whole order' threat, as I had not mentioned this possibility to my parents and it would cause them great inconvenience, but hopefully it wouldn't come to that.

It didn't!

Within an hour a customer service supervisor had called to advise that one of their fitters would be sent out with a replacement 400mm wall unit that very afternoon. I couldn't help thinking; "I wonder what will arrive this time?"

As it happened the fitter brought the correct unit, was extremely pleasant, taking time to check that it matched the rest of the units, and he apologised for all the trouble we had experienced.

While this helped, the correct microwave oven was never supplied, apparently having gone out of stock and been discontinued since my parents had placed their order! They finally settled on a different model but could get no compensation for the inconvenience and disappointment caused. As the company pointed out, they had collected the unwanted microwave and subsequently delivered the (slightly) more expensive model chosen by my parents, *at no extra cost!* This, in their opinion, was sufficient compensation!

Our confidence in this company remains seriously damaged.

Care to be different?

When a problem occurs, what makes you appreciate someone taking it off your shoulders?

Why do you think this problem went on so long?

Which of the Customer Service representatives should have taken responsibility to sort this problem out?

What do you think of the service provided by the fitter who arrived with the correct unit at the end of the story?

On reflection, are there occasions when you think you should have taken on responsibility to sort certain situations out?

Taking responsibility to resolve a problem will usually add to your workload, so exactly what aspects of taking on a problem can be enjoyable?

Care to be different?
- enjoy taking a problem off someone's shoulders

Notes...

6

Enjoy giving
a little extra

Off limits
-that's not my job

There's a common phrase which talks about 'going the extra mile'. We might use it to compliment someone who has gone out of their way to be helpful. But two things strike me about this phrase. Firstly, we should be updating it to 'going the extra kilometre'. And secondly, mile or kilometre, how do you know that's enough? Maybe we should be willing to go two or three kilometres. On the other hand would 100 metres perhaps suffice?

Of course, the principle behind the phrase is a willingness to do more than necessary, in the interests of being helpful to others, and making them happy. I like the sound of that, and here's an occasion when I was very grateful to see it in action...

~~~~~~

Our office was very busy! We were stretched to our limits, preparing information for a visit from an important customer, when it became clear that there was no way we could complete compilation of all the required data in time. Our customer was a demanding lady, and although we could think of a few excuses, we knew they would not go down well. One way or another, we needed to find a way of presenting her with what she wanted.

One of my colleagues stepped up to the mark: "This is clearly a classic case for introducing a brainstorming session!"

It began enthusiastically enough, but after having deliberated on our ideas for around thirty minutes, we came up with nothing, other than the realisation that we had thirty minutes less than we had before, to achieve our impossible task. If only we had a few more pairs of hands, we mused.

It was then that the miracle happened... another department offered help!

Co-operation *within* departments had improved dramatically over a number of years, but helpfulness *between* departments was a comparatively new initiative, approached by the majority of employees with a fair degree of caution.

There were also a small number of hard-core, anti-change campaigners who opposed inter-departmental co-operation with a vengeance. This small group, who did not in any sense work together 'as a group', included some very strong and influential characters. Most of them were hard-workers, but they had a core belief that change was 'out to get them'. So they opposed it.

Tom was one of these characters.

He was well aware of the pressure on our office that day. Indeed, he had no small part to play in contributing to it. Not that he'd done anything wrong – he had been under a lot of pressure himself over the last few weeks. But Tom was well aware that the reports he had only just submitted, were causing a reworking of a lot of the data required by our important customer. Despite this knowledge, it probably didn't even occur to him to offer help.

In Tom's mind, departmental boundaries should not be crossed. To do so would be like stepping outside of an army shelter and exposing yourself to gunfire. Tom's department was his world, his security, and he would fight at all costs to protect it from invasion. Anyone who mildly threatened his position, could find themselves on the receiving end of an intimidating vocal attack, accompanied by a display of angry gestures.

Some found Tom's attitude frustrating; others laughed at his 'old-fashioned' views, but Tom was deadly serious. His deeply ingrained belief system had served him well for years – in his opinion – and he was not going to give it up "in favour of the latest half-baked, unproven, flavour-of-the-month, management idea!" as he delicately put it.

Ollie often worked with Tom. He had been in the same department for three years, and although they got along fairly well, Ollie didn't share Tom's views on departmental boundaries.

Ollie enjoyed his job, and appreciated knowing the parameters of his responsibilities; what was expected of him. However, he also believed in helping others to do their jobs well, where possible; 'Internal Customer Service', as the bosses liked to call it. Ollie simply saw it as being pleasant to people and engaging in a bit of 'give and take', with a bit more emphasis on the 'give'. He strongly felt that if everyone worked that way, life would be more pleasant. But not being a pushy type, he largely kept his views to himself.

But not today!

Ollie had become aware of our problem over a chance discussion at the coffee machine. I had not seen him arrive behind me, and with my mind still focused on trying to draw some sort of positive morsel from our otherwise fruitless brainstorming session, I had whisked away from the machine and turned straight into him. Ollie immediately lent a hand clearing up the spilt coffee, during which I explained the background behind my apparent clumsiness.

As he became aware of the size of the task we were facing, Ollie was quick to reach a conclusion: "You're just not going to be able to do it", he declared.

I was about to thank him for his insightful summary of the situation, but was pleasantly surprised when he prevented me from doing so. "Let me see if I can get our department to help", he continued, and he was gone.

I was left pondering over the notion that the brainstorming had in fact contributed to a possible solution…

Within half an hour our two departments were focused on a common cause. With some quickly considered decisions, merging of responsibility was established and the task became more manageable as we worked together to increase the checking and research necessary.

Although the nature of the work gave rise to some difficulties in sharing equipment and work spaces, most people were very helpful and willing to give ground. But true to form, Tom went out of his way to defend his possessions and space with an unnecessary degree of ferocity.

The job was completed in good time and our customer left expressing her appreciation!

Because several people were willing to do a little more than they necessarily had to, no-one had to bear too much strain, and the end result was pleasing all round.

And that was also the day that Ollie gained a new-found respect amongst his colleagues, not to mention a new-found confidence in himself. He became increasingly adept at taking a lead to do what he believed to be right, and people admired his conviction and courage. Over time he became as strong and influential as Tom, who sadly, despite being a solid and reliable hard-worker, remained very ingrained in his ways.

Care to be different?

Who do you most identify with in this story and why?

Do you think Tom had any reasonable grounds for taking the position he did? To what extent do you think boundaries are important, to stop you being drawn into all kinds of work which you don't have time to do?

How much do you agree or disagree with Ollie's views, summarised below?

> "Ollie believed in helping others to do their jobs well, where possible... engaging in a bit of 'give and take', with a bit more emphasis on the 'give'. He strongly felt that if everyone worked that way, life would be more pleasant."

What does the term 'Internal Customer Service', mean to you? How important is it in your organisation?

How much do you feel someone like Tom limits their own potential to enjoy work and life?

If you were Ollie, what would you have said to Tom to help him think the situation through?

Care to be different?
- enjoy giving a little extra

Notes...

7

Enjoy making and keeping promises

Don't take our word for it
- how to raise and shatter expectations

How often have you been let down by a broken promise? More times than you can count I expect. It's very easy to make a promise, and in the vast majority of cases, the person making a promise fully intends to keep it. So why are so many broken? And is that just something we have to put up with?

I don't know about you, but I don't like it when a promise is broken, especially when it's broken with a blatant disregard for the fact that it was made in the first place – which is exactly what happened when I went on a simple shopping expedition...

~~~~~~~~~~~~~~~~~~~~~~~~~~~~~~~~~~~~

It was mid-May when I came across the voucher I had been given for Christmas. It wasn't high value, but I had totally forgotten about it, so it was a pleasant surprise – almost like I'd received it twice!

The downside was that I would have to make a visit into town. I'm a reluctant shopper, finding the whole process rather daunting. This may seem strange to the regular shopper, and those who shop as a hobby, but for me it is out of my comfort zone. Invariably something awkward or embarrassing happens, increasing my resistance to making a further trip until absolutely necessary.

Nevertheless, the next day, I determined to make my way into town to spend my voucher.

I found a parking space with ease, and negotiated the lift into the shopping centre without incident. I began to meander in a 'shopping-like' manner, trying to mingle unnoticed with the confident, purposeful majority. I noted that several stores had disappeared since my last visit, and a few new ones had arrived in their place.

As I turned a corner to see the clothes store with the name that matched my voucher, I was pleased to note that it was still there, but also had an uncomfortable sense that things were going too smoothly.

I need not have worried!

After some 20 minutes of looking for a suitable purchase, I'm sorry to say that the only item I had in my hand was a pack of vests. Not the most exciting selection, but in the absence of any other item taking my fancy, I concluded that vests would always come in useful. Everyone should have a spare vest or two at the back of their wardrobe, just in case. At least, that's what my mother always used to say, and obviously it stuck! Armed with my voucher, and my mundane warming garments, I approached the checkout to make the exchange.

But then I remembered... gloves! Woollen gloves!!

Perhaps it was a link to the cosy feelings of wearing a warm vest in winter; maybe it was the hand of the manikin that fell to the floor as I passed by... possibly it was the poster of a sheep wearing a woollen jumper (which I was looking at when I made brief contact with said manikin); whatever it was that triggered my memory, suddenly my need of woolen gloves leapt to the forefront of my mind with some force.

It was three winters previously that I had first purchased a pair of woollen gloves. It was exactly three days after that purchase, that my right hand glove had been unceremoniously snatched from my person by a hyperactive species of ape!

Although the 'safari' incident has provided everyone with a jolly good laugh at my expense, both on the day, and on numerous occasions since, it's not so funny for me when I have to scrape ice off the car at seven o'clock in the morning!

During each and every spell of cold weather, I'd developed the habit of saying to myself: "I'll buy a new pair of gloves next time I go into town". But on each of the infrequent town-visits made, I had never remembered to do so. Until now! I determined there and then to furnish myself with a pair of woollen gloves.

But it was mid-May, and I could not find gloves anywhere. Socks, socks, and more socks, in all manner of colours and designs. But gloves? No. I was disappointed.

It entered my mind to ask for help, but being male, I rejected that temptation and instead launched into an even more thorough and systematic search of the entire store.

In the end, having returned once again to the socks, I had no choice; night was closing in and my resolve was weakening. "Excuse me," I ventured to a passing assistant, "Could you point me in the direction of the glove department?"

I don't know why I said 'department'; I was just trying to sound casual and that's the way it came out.

"I'm sorry sir, we don't have any gloves in the store at the moment – this is the Spring range". The assistant's expression contained a mixture of amusement and pity, with a hint of disdain.

Fired up by embarrassment and an instinctive desire to regain credibility, I found myself speaking again, with the only thing that came to mind; "Er… the sock department, sorry, I mean the sock department."

"Okay," the assistant spoke slowly, and was clearly making an assessment of my sanity, "That's just behind you sir." Of course it was.

I was acutely aware that I had regained no credibility whatsoever. I mumbled an embarrassed thank you to the assistant and turned to the socks, picking up a pack of five pairs in assorted colours. I observed that they were made of wool, from which I seemed to draw some illogical degree of comfort, and decided to keep them.

However, I now faced the dilemma of whether to substantially supplement the value of my voucher and splash out on both items, or walk through the whole store again to return the vests to their respective shelf.

While pondering this surprisingly difficult decision, my attention was caught by a sign attached to an adjacent pillar. It read:

"Special 30% discount on all woollen goods - today only".

"Things are looking up", I mused, and made my decision. Now armed with my voucher, vests, *and* woollen socks, I confidently approached the checkout, looking forward to a happy conclusion to my visit.

I offered up my purchases for bar code reading and held out my voucher in readiness. "That will be £26.99", announced the disinterested individual behind the 'service desk'. A disinterested hand reached towards my voucher but I was quick to withdraw it. "That price doesn't include the discount", I said. The reply was prompt, if curt: "What discount?"

"I believe today is the day for a special 30% discount on woollen goods," I replied pleasantly.

"That was yesterday," the assistant retorted, without any indication of interest as to why I might have thought otherwise.

"But there's a sign saying it's today", I informed her, with a helpful glance towards the pillar.

"No, it was yesterday. If there's a sign up now it should have been taken down. Isn't that right Sara?" From the adjacent check out, Sara offered a slight nod of the head while continuing to inspect her nails.

"There it is sir!" My sales assistant retained an arrogant confidence and clearly had no intention of entertaining the matter further. The appearance of the word 'sir' in her response, which could have been taken to indicate a certain level of respect, clearly had no such significance.

"But surely if your advertising is telling me ..." I remonstrated. "No, it was yesterday", came the increasingly abrupt response. Then, more as a threat than an offer of help, she inquired: "Do you want me to call the manager?"

"No", I replied despondently; given the amount of money involved, I decided not to become embroiled in further dispute and reluctantly surrendered my voucher.

Something about the way she had offered an interaction with 'the manager,' had made me feel I would only be subjecting myself to extended argument which would prove both frustrating and fruitless.

Handing over the required cash balance, I waited in silence as my now 'expensive' vests and woollen socks were unceremoniously ushered into a plastic bag sporting the store's logo. Underneath the logo were the words: *"Always something extra for our customers"*.

I felt cheated as I left the store.

Glancing over my shoulder, in a wistful manner that would have graced the ending of a melancholy film, I observed the 30% discount sign being hastily removed.

Care to be different?

What exactly is a promise? How often do we make them?

How do you feel when someone keeps a promise made to you? How do you feel when you keep a promise made to someone else?

Given that the promise in the story was on a sign, who exactly made the promise and who was responsible for fulfilling it?

If you were one of the shop assistants, how would you have handled the situation differently? What if you'd been there all day, were tired and wanted to go home?

Why do so many people break promises?

Does it matter if you break a promise? Is it different if the promise you are breaking was made by someone else in your organisation?

How easily do you make promises, and then find you are unable or unwilling to carry them out?

Would you like to change anything about the way you go about making and keeping promises?

Care to be different?
- enjoy making and keeping promises

Notes...

8

Enjoy treating people with consideration

Passing the baton
- when customers are inconvenient

For a top-notch relay team, 'passing the baton' efficiently is the very essence of what they are about. At a school sports day however (certainly in my case) a relay race can take on the form of comic disaster. Most of us saw the baton as something we did not want to be holding and sought to part company with it at the earliest opportunity, which often resulted in it being dropped to the ground! Sadly, it is true to say that customers are often passed around like that unwanted baton...

Sometimes people ask for unreasonable things, or perhaps more accurately, *inconvenient* things. Do you ever get the feeling that customers are interrupting your day? Can they not understand this? And could they not be more considerate about the implications of requests they make to you? The sooner they are off your radar the better, then you can get on with whatever it is that you need, or want, to do.

I've known Mike for many years; he's a good friend, with a seemingly unlimited supply of funny stories to tell. He's not an unreasonable person, but his request in this story was certainly *inconvenient*...

~~~~~~

Mike and his family are keen campers. At least, Mike is, and his family go with him. That's wife, Janice, and five assorted children. The year they decided to go to Scotland proved to be the adventure that Mike had promised, although not entirely in the way he had planned it!

Settling down for the 975 kilometre journey, the family set off on their expedition; seven of them in their large people carrier, their caravan and copious amounts of assorted equipment in tow. It was 9.30am.

At 9.50am, some fifteen kilometres from their home, the vehicle's engine spluttered and failed to function. Despite the heavy load, this was a vehicle designed for heavy duty work, and Mike was not impressed with the lacklustre performance, especially as it left him travelling without power in the middle lane of a three-lane carriageway.

Remaining calm and composed, Mike managed to use the accumulated momentum of car, passengers, caravan and equipment to safely manoeuvre to the side of the road. Momentarily, Mike saw himself as the captain of a distressed aircraft who had just landed his charge under extreme conditions. As the vehicle rolled to a stop, he relaxed back in his seat, anticipating the compliments that would undoubtedly be flowing in his direction. But none were forthcoming.

Although free of compliments, the airwaves were rapidly filled with questions:

"What's happened Dad?"
"Why have we stopped?"
"What now!?"

"Is there something wrong with the car?"
And the inevitable: "Are we there yet?"

"I'm going to take a look at the engine", Mike proclaimed. In truth, this was more about removing himself from the tirade of questions, than with any real conviction that his inspection would be productive. He knew which end of the car the engine was situated, but that was about it.

Mike walked confidently to the front of the car, paused to take a cursory glance underneath the vehicle for effect, then spent an embarrassing two minutes fiddling with the bonnet release catch. The six faces peering at him from the other side of the windscreen were distinctly unnerving, and Mike did not appreciate the knowing smirks prevalent on some! Eventually, more by luck than judgement, the catch gave way to his insistent prodding. Raising the bonnet, he was grateful that the array of expectant, enquiring faces were no longer visible.

Mike propped the bonnet into place and double-checked the prop mechanism, to avoid the further complication of a premature closure onto his head. It had happened before... but not today.

There were a few things under the bonnet that Mike recognised but he had no real knowledge of how anything worked. He wiggled a few electrical wires, prodded a few things he didn't recognise, and checked the level of liquid in the windscreen washer bottle. He then assumed a hunched position over the engine, staring at it thoughtfully, and nodding as he considered his next step.

He was trying to gauge a balance between giving up too quickly, and the impression of ineptness that would be portrayed by an overly-long inspection that produced no result.

In reality his deliberations were futile. His older passengers knew his incompetence in these matters, having been subjected to a number of previous demonstrations, and the younger passengers were still of a mind that Dad was brilliant at everything. He decided to take small comfort from the incomplete insight of his younger passengers and returned to the driver's seat.

"We'll need to phone for assistance", Mike announced, as if his preceding inspection had been instrumental in reaching this conclusion. Most of his passengers knew the five minutes or so he had spent in front of the car, had only served to delay the arrival of such assistance by an equal amount of time. But they indulged him in his need to portray a level of competence greater than existed, and all maintained comparative silence while the necessary call was made.

The rescue service arrived within fifteen minutes. Mike turned to his passengers with an expression designed to take some credit for the speed with which this had occurred. Not for the first time that day, he was on a different wavelength. Most faces returned an expression that indicated they were already fed up with waiting.

"Soon be on our way now", he commented, getting out of the car. It was a simple statement of hope on his part. The truth of the matter was going to be far more complicated.

The trained technician soon declared that the heavily loaded vehicle was going no further until the engine was subjected to serious repair. "But don't worry", he said confidently, "We'll soon get you home".

Mike felt a gathering gloom descend over him. How was he going to break the news to the rest of the party that they would not, after all, be going anywhere. At least, not today.

Personal pride was also at stake! Mike was responsible for travel arrangements, and his vehicle's disappointing performance was reflecting poorly on his own capabilities. He made a decision, and addressed the technician: "Actually, we don't want to go home. We're on our way to Scotland and we'd like to continue to our destination".

The technician pondered the situation, studying Mike's face as if to check whether he was being serious. Mike had faithfully paid his annual subscription for the breakdown company's 'full package' for several years, including the recovery option to a choice of 'home' or 'destination'; now he wanted to cash in, big time! He was serious.

Checking the precise, and remote destination within Scotland that Mike wished to go to, the technician consulted his map. "That's probably close on a thousand kilometres, sir", he said, with a tone that clearly questioned the wisdom of Mike's request.

"We'll need to arrange special transport for this lot", the technician continued, with no small degree of reluctance, "But if that's what you want to do?"

If that was an attempt to make Mike feel guilty about putting them to the trouble of arranging the necessary transport, it wasn't working.

"We want to go to Scotland!" Mike was unmoved. This was what he and his family wanted to do.

This was the last time he was to feel such strength of conviction, but this was the point of decision, and the full weight of the organisation's recovery operation was about to be triggered into action.

"Okay" The technician said it with an air of resignation, coupled with a hint of, "I hope you know what you're doing", and began to put the wheels in motion, literally.

Mike returned to his family to deliver the good news!

The atmosphere inside the family vehicle had become tense and disagreeable. Mike's first thought was, "How inconsiderate!" After all, he was the one sorting everything out. All they had to do was sit and wait. If this was the state of play after half-an-hour of waiting around, how were they going to cope with the further wait while recovery transport was sorted!?

Before he could do anything with it, Mike's first thought was slowly pushed aside by the gradual emergence of his second thought, which was more troubling. He had not consulted with any of his passengers about the decision he had just made; one passenger in particular.

Too late, he mused, and announced the action he had taken!

The children, aged from four to sixteen, were all in their own way excited at the prospect of being towed by a very large breakdown truck. This enthusiasm would be short-lived, but for now Mike took it at face value.

His wife, on the other hand, displayed no enthusiasm whatsoever. Janice's face seemed to indicate a state of shock more than anything else, but at least she was silent, and Mike was happy to take that, for now.

It had already begun to occur to Mike that there were downsides to traveling into the heart of Scotland on a breakdown truck. Namely, it would take considerably longer, and they would still be in possession of a broken-down vehicle in an area which may not be flush with repair options.

Mike hoped these points would escape his wife's attention for the time being.

But, slowly and surely, she began to find words to describe her incredulousness in respect of his decision. Janice listed the downsides Mike had thought of, and several more. Mike felt it was unhelpful of her to go through this list in front of the children, but also felt it would be unhelpful to point it out. So he didn't.

After a further forty minutes of waiting, during which Janice's list of downsides had grown even longer, two more recovery vehicles arrived: a minibus to carry the seven-strong party, and a winch-truck to tow the broken-down vehicle away. The caravan was duly hitched onto the tow-hook of the original recovery vehicle, and eventually the whole convoy began to move. The children had not enjoyed the forty minute wait but were now once again caught up with a sense of adventure; this was still not shared by Janice.

"Finally on our way then!", Mike proclaimed with all the enthusiasm he could muster. He deliberately looked in the direction of the youngest member of his party, who duly obliged with a look of admiration.

All went well for approximately two kilometres, at which point all three vehicles left the main carriageway, and started heading up a road which was actually taking them in the wrong direction. Mike pointed this out to the minibus driver, who merely commented that they were being taken to a holding centre. The driver's disinterested manner indicated he would not welcome further conversation, so Mike obliged with an uneasy silence, occasionally smiling encouragingly at his kids, and apologetically towards Janice, who was shaking her head from side to side in a continued state of disbelief.

On arrival at the holding centre, the family proceeded to dismount from the minibus, while the driver moaned to a colleague about how inconvenient the call-out had been, due to it interrupting his viewing of an important football match. Mike inadvertently began to apologise for the poor timing of their breakdown, until he picked up the intense, "What do you think you are doing?" glare from Janice. Turning his attention to an area map on the wall, Mike realised that they were now further away from their destination than they had been when they had left home over two hours ago. It was a fact he elected to keep to himself.

The holding centre was a large warehouse, containing several small recovery vehicles and a small variety of stacked goods along one wall. Mike and his family were ushered into a small makeshift office come 'rest' room and left to their own devices. It was not very restful.

There was a coffee machine from which Mike purchased a dubious refreshment for Janice, and a largely empty snack machine containing just three bags of crisps. Mike extracted these with some difficulty, on account of the machine questioning the validity of his coinage, and placed them on the solitary desk for sharing.

Leaving Janice to deal with the finer details of how three bags of crisps can be effectively shared between five children, Mike took his leave in search of further information.

The place was largely deserted, but he did find two individuals in another makeshift office near the entrance. They were able to confirm that a special flat-back breakdown truck, with a very large cabin capacity, had been requested for the mammoth task of transporting Mike, his car, his caravan, and his family, but as yet they could not advise an arrival time.

Mike asked if there was anywhere he could buy provisions for his family. It was as if he had enquired about the possibility of a brief trip to the moon! They looked at each other doubtfully and shook their heads: "Not really mate, no".

Armed with no real additional information, Mike returned to the 'crisp sharing' scene and found things had been organised rather well. The approving glance he offered to his wife was returned with a look he knew well. "No thanks to you", was the basic sentiment.

They all settled down to waiting, feeling very much like the stacked commodities lined up along the wall; insignificant objects, uncertain of their fate.

The family remained marooned in this state of limbo for over two hours. Mike made intermittent trips to the front office to gather what little information was available, and then returned to receive a further dose of moaning, complaining and disapproval.

Just as Mike's popularity was hitting an all-time low, the family heard the very loud roar of an engine. It was a roar they would become uncomfortably familiar with over the next several hours, but for now it was a welcome sound.

They emerged from their holding store and watched as their inoperative vehicle and caravan were duly winched onto the back of a massive truck. They were then informed there would be a further twenty minute wait for a new driver. The burst of noise and activity was replaced with a familiar silence, and the family filed back into their storage room to savour its aesthetic virtues one last time.

Finally, they were collected from the store, loaded into the extensive cabin and their long journey to Scotland began!

The driver was not unfriendly, but not talkative either. Mike presumed he had just become used to transporting vehicles and 'livestock' around the country, and was simply focused on carrying out his job of moving Mike and his family to the destination specified on his paperwork.

Unfortunately, this destination was not Scotland.

Due to the nature of 'the system', there are area borders within which vehicles and drivers work, and it was therefore necessary for the party to be passed on yet again. So it was, that somewhere south of the Scottish border, their driver unloaded his cargo in a warehouse not unlike the holding centre they had frequented earlier that day, and drove off!

The waiting started again. The novelty of breakdown trucks had long since worn off, and each and every one of the children were now becoming fractious in their own special ways.

Pleasingly, Janice had bestowed conditional forgiveness upon Mike, and was doing her tired best to help him keep spirits up. Mike was not quite sure what all the conditions were, but reasoned he would find out in due course. For the time being it was good to have her support.

Eventually, the family was picked up by another driver who duly loaded and transported the entire 'package', before depositing it at its final destination, in the middle of a field, at 3.00am in the morning.

The family's anticipated eleven hour journey, interspersed with pleasant, well-planned refreshment breaks, had been transformed into a marathon eighteen hour cargo shipment!

Their 3.00am arrival on site was announced by the throbbing engine of the enormous breakdown truck, and the clanking of the winch as it worked to remove first their caravan and then their stricken motor, from the host vehicle onto the field.

If this had not been enough to wake all other campers up, the retracting winch certainly was. With unloading complete, it was unceremoniously recoiled at full speed by the driver, causing it to bounce across the surface of the flat-back truck and crash into its off-duty position like a resounding gong!

Seemingly oblivious to the decibels being generated, the driver revved up and made his noisy departure, leaving the family to face the music in the morning.

Fortunately, the good spirits of fellow campers prevailed, and many were keen listeners to Mike's tale of woe, related many times over the following days. It took five days to get the sick vehicle repaired, after which the family resumed enjoyment of their two week holiday, more in line with their original plan.

When Mike initially told me this story, complete with the amusing insights into his mind, I simply enjoyed a good laugh. But on reflection I thought about how little time the family actually spent laughing on the day all this occurred. Obviously the breakdown and a certain amount of delay were unavoidable, but what really got to me is how the family were treated like commodities. People don't like being treated as commodities - because it's unpleasant, discomforting, and at times humiliating. Mike and his family were on the receiving end of all that!

Then I realised something really important.

No one set out to treat Mike and his family that way. People were just doing their jobs and didn't realise the impact their actions were having on others.

It struck me how easy it is to inadvertently treat people like commodities! And despite best intentions, I could see that sometimes I had been guilty of doing exactly the same thing!

Care to be different?

What do you think of Mike's request to be towed to Scotland? Was he being unreasonable?

How well do you think Mike's wife handled the situation? Was she unhelpful, or did Mike get off lightly?

How do you think Mike and his family were treated? If you were one of the relay team, what would you have done differently?

Have you ever treated people like commodities without realising it? What causes this?

What are the best ways of making people feel looked after and cared for?

"Treat your customer as you would like to be treated yourself." Is this a good rule of thumb? When might it not be?

Reflecting on the last few days, how would you rate the level of consideration demonstrated by you to people you have interacted with?

How much enjoyment can be created by considerate behaviour?

Care to be different?
- enjoy treating people with consideration

Notes...

Part 3
Things you may find helpful, interesting and perhaps enjoyable

Deciding to be cheerful
– some practical tips and ideas to help you into the right frame of mind

Sometimes the apparently insurmountable is conquered by surprisingly simple actions!

'Being cheerful' is easier said than done! Of course it is. But if you are willing to carry out simple actions which can lift your state of mind, you will often be surprised at the results that flow from your efforts!

So here are some ideas. Why not approach them with an open mind and give them a try:

- Enjoy doing something for someone else
- Enjoy trying something new
- Enjoy exploring and experimenting
- Enjoy your successes
- Enjoy focusing on someone else – ask them how they're doing
- Enjoy smiling when you meet people
- Enjoy a photo of someone who makes you happy
- Enjoy a picture, photo or other visual reminder of a happy memory
- Enjoy appreciating things you may have previously not noticed or taken for granted
- Enjoy learning new information

- Enjoy saying "Thank you"
- Enjoy writing a letter to someone you've not seen for a while
- Enjoy focusing on your goal and why it's important to you
- Enjoy listening to your favourite uplifting music
- Enjoy exercise – be creative in finding ways to exercise
- Enjoy reading or watching something that makes you laugh
- Enjoy spending time with friends who lift your spirits

And of course, enjoy giving great customer service!

Are your feelings of enjoyment worth fighting for?

YES! OF COURSE THEY ARE!

So when things don't go so well – hold on to your decision to 'Be cheerful', and determine to return to that disposition as soon as possible. However tough things get for you, don't let people or circumstances stop you enjoying *your* work and *your* life.

Choose simple actions that suit *you*, and take steps to 'Be cheerful'!

Deciding to enjoy giving great customer service

– a quick-reference summary of the eight easy ways to make life more enjoyable for you and your customers

1   *Enjoy making people feel comfortable*

2   *Enjoy putting 'heart' into your words and actions*

3   *Enjoy being sensitive to someone's situation and feelings*

4   *Enjoy being 'on the ball'*

5   *Enjoy taking a problem off someone's shoulders*

6   *Enjoy giving a little extra*

7   *Enjoy making and keeping promises*

8   *Enjoy treating people with consideration*

Good customer service is an 'attitude of quality', expressed in all I think, say, and do

An 'attitude of quality' is a desire to get things right for the benefit of my customer

Make it *your* decision to *enjoy* giving great customer service

Allow yourself to *enjoy* the process *and* the results

A learning opportunity based on 'Care to be different?'

– introducing the 'ENJOY' customer relationship programme

'ENJOY'

......is the attitudinal customer relationship programme from Keyturn Training, that puts a smile of satisfaction on everybody's face!

......is the unique training programme built around the content of this book!

Using 'Care to be different?' as a foundation, the 'ENJOY' training experience adds light and colour to the key points of this book, inspiring and equipping people to enjoy providing great customer service!

'ENJOY'

......is founded on attitudinal principles, which enable individuals to increasingly enjoy their work, and in particular to gain pleasure from helping others ('customers' of all types)

......recognises that the reward of enjoyment fuels desire to give great service

......ignites desire, builds motivation and strengthens resolve, to ensure all types of 'customer' are well-satisfied!

......lifts individual desire into collective desire: the strongest foundation on which to build a robust, high-performing customer focused culture, that will stand the test of time

......delivers consistent high levels of 'World Class' customer service, customer satisfaction and customer retention

---

Keyturn Training Limited, Inner Lodge, Dunchurch Park, Rugby Road, Dunchurch, Rugby, Warwickshire, United Kingdom, CV22 6QW

Tel: 01788 815500; Fax: 01788 816662;
Email: pjm@keyturn-training.co.uk; www.keyturn-training.co.uk

More about Keyturn Training
- an introduction to other learning opportunities

Keyturn Training was established in 1990 and has grown to become one of the leading training and development companies within the UK, as well as working further afield for international clients.

Keyturn are specialists in the art of customer service and offer a range of tailored services to assist individuals, teams, or whole organisations in developing strong customer relationships.

Keyturn also provide comprehensive and highly commended training in the following areas:
- management development
- supervisor development
- personal development

The common link in all Keyturn's activity is in 'achieving results through people'.

Keyturn's priority is developing people so that they are more able to do the jobs which they are employed to do, gaining greater job satisfaction in the process; in turn, this produces higher levels of motivation and achievement.

Through our uniquely designed approach, participants on Keyturn programmes focus their learning on achieving results from the earliest stages of engagement through to seeing real changes taking place in their working environment.

And as you would expect, there is always a strong focus on enjoying the whole process of learning, as well as enjoying the fulfilment gained from putting it into practice!

Every year, Keyturn run hundreds of successful learning and development programmes for a diverse client range, including many high profile names. We deliver relevant, down-to-earth training that is flexible, interactive, enjoyable, and immediately effective. Our team of training professionals, supported by a highly efficient project management team, together provide unrivalled levels of customer service!

Keyturn Training Limited, Inner Lodge, Dunchurch Park, Rugby Road, Dunchurch, Rugby, Warwickshire, United Kingdom, CV22 6QW

Tel: 01788 815500; Fax: 01788 816662;
Email: pjm@keyturn-training.co.uk; www.keyturn-training.co.uk

'The unluckiest customer In the world'
– a taster of the next book from Philip Maggs

To be fair, from Colin's perspective, his enquiry to Carol was only made after a considerable attempt on his part to make sense of the various information offered on product packaging. He had loitered in the plumbing aisle for some twenty minutes, fully appreciating the need to avoid bothering staff within the store unnecessarily.

However, when Carol strode confidently down the very aisle he was deliberating in, he had observed a sense of purpose and authority about this lady, that indicated a level of experience and responsibility which he would undoubtedly benefit from tapping into.

Plucking up courage to present his question without appearing to be an incompetent novice, Colin took a few steps forward and stood politely beside the intensely focused individual.

Wrapped up in the frustration she was feeling towards James, Carol had swept down the aisle without even noticing Colin's presence, let alone the consternation written across his face as he tried to unravel the possibilities of connecting one product to another. As he walked up to her she remained oblivious. Hence when he spoke, and made her jump, Carol's perception was that he had simply 'appeared' at her shoulder.

Before her brain was in gear and prepared to receive any communication at all, Colin's rather jumbled query had been emitted, and his words made even less sense than they would have done ordinarily.

Carol did not intend to respond in an abrupt, aggressive or unhelpful manner (rude, if we are being honest) but it just came out in a single word: "*What!?*"

It's quite incredible to consider how much emotion can be packed with such impact into a single word. But it can! And Colin felt it now. It was a defining moment.

A different type of character may have snapped back, or sought assistance elsewhere, or lodged some form of complaint. But Colin, in his quiet vulnerable way, simply found himself feeling like an incompetent novice – the very scenario he had been keen to avoid.

Uncertain of how to rephrase his question with any greater clarity, and even more uncertain of a welcoming response, he found himself muttering half-sentences along the lines of: "It doesn't matter", and "I'll leave it for now".

Blissfully unaware of the way her, "*What!?*" had impacted on Colin, Carol's irritated glare only served to reinforce his instinctive reluctance to take the matter further and in the interests of survival he first stepped back, then made his exit from the aisle, swiftly followed by an exit from the store – without making his plumbing purchase, or returning to look at the power tool offers which had caught his eye some twenty minutes earlier.

Carol continued to rearrange the plumbing stock with a degree of force that somewhat exceeded the amount required for the job, still shaking her head at the weird customer who had crept up on her, made her jump, mumbled in a confused manner, and then wandered off again! Clearly the man had not seriously wanted anything in the first place. Carol mused how often customers approached her without first clearly thinking through what they actually want!

Arriving home somewhat disappointed that his budding enthusiasm for 'Do-It-Yourself' home maintenance had been thwarted, Colin picked up the telephone number of the plumber his neighbour had recommended. He called the number and left a message on the answer-phone, which promised a response within two hours.

While attempting to remain positive, Colin's despondent demeanour made him doubt whether this promise would be kept. He waited for four hours, keeping a close eye on the leaky radiator valve which had come to his attention early that morning while he was brushing his teeth. The phone did not ring. The promise was not kept.

Despite this disappointing, or rather non-existent response from the recommended plumber, Colin took heart from the fact that the leak appeared no worse than it was when he had first noticed it. He confidently estimated that it would be at least 24 hours before the slow drip would fill the rather large breakfast bowl he had placed beneath the offending joint. With no reason to be concerned he began to prepare for work.

Closing his front door, Colin left to do his nightshift. This was precisely the moment the leaky valve had been waiting for!

Assuming an evil personality, which inanimate objects are sometimes temporarily capable of, it listened intensely as Colin got into his car, reversed out of the drive, and disappeared down the street. Then, it struck!!

If you would like to be notified of the publication of

'The unluckiest customer in the world',

please send an email to pjm@keyturn-training.co.uk as follows:

Subject: The unluckiest customer in the world

Message: Please notify me of publication

Keyturn Training Limited, Inner Lodge, Dunchurch Park, Rugby Road, Dunchurch, Rugby, Warwickshire, United Kingdom, CV22 6QW

Tel: 01788 815500; Fax: 01788 816662;
Email: pjm@keyturn-training.co.uk; www.keyturn-training.co.uk